First published in 1992
in the United States by
Gloucester Press Inc.
95 Madison Avenue
New York, NY 10016

Library of Congress Cataloging-in-Publication Data

Hodge, Anthony.
    Collage / by Anthony Hodge.
      p.   cm. -- (Hands on arts and crafts)
    Includes index.
    Summary: Uses a series of simple projects to
present a variety of collage techniques.
    ISBN 0-531-17323-2 (lib. bdg.)
    1. Collage--Technique--Juvenile literature. [1.
Collage--Technique. 2. Art--Technique.] I. Title. II.
Series: Hodge, Anthony. Hands on arts and crafts.
N7433.7.H63   1992
702'.8'12--dc20   91-34408   CIP   AC

Printed in Belgium

The author, Anthony Hodge, is an artist whose work is
regularly exhibited. He has taught art to adults and
children for 20 years.

Design: Rob Hillier and Andy Wilkinson
Editor: Jen Green
Collages by Anthony Hodge
Illustrations by Ron Hayward Associates

COLLAGE

Anthony Hodge

Gloucester Press
New York · London · Toronto · Sydney

CONTENTS

INTRODUCTION

Collage, a French word meaning pasting or gluing, is a very flexible art form. It can take you beyond the limitations of paints and brushes, and introduce you to a new world of creative picture making.

Everyone can do it
Collage can be quick and easy. It makes use of ready-made materials like photographs and colored paper, and is good for anyone who enjoys making images. You don't have to be a great artist to produce spectacular results. Collage can go hand in hand with drawing and painting, or can be a separate activity in its own right.

New from old
Collage is cheap. Rather than demanding expensive new equipment, it makes use of things people often think of as garbage. The materials you need are all around you and can cost next to nothing. Collage is about combining familiar things in new and original ways.

About this book
This book begins with a guide to tools, techniques and materials. With the aid of projects, it guides you through simple image-making to a series of more advanced techniques.

▷ *"Scraps of styrofoam and candy box paper suggested this snow scene. I used corrugated cardboard for the house and string for the plants and broomstick. I laid bubble wrap packing material over blue paper to get the effect of falling snow."*

TEARING AND CUTTING

The next pages introduce some basic tools and techniques for paper collage. To get paper to the shape you require, you will need to tear or cut it. There are many different ways of accomplishing even this first step.

Tearing

It is very simple to pick up a piece of paper and tear a shape out of it. A torn edge can look very pleasing, both on its own or when placed next to a cut edge. Torn paper can often look surprisingly effective, once you've placed it in position. For more hints on tearing techniques, see the Practical Tips section on page 31.

Cutting

The main tools for cutting are scissors and craft knives. Scissors are relatively safe and easy to control. Used skillfully, they can produce a variety of curved and straight lines.

A craft knife can be used to cut lines more freely. Used with care, a knife can cut shapes in paper as easily as a pencil can draw them. A craft knife is sharp. Cut away from your body, and be careful not to cut your other hand, which is holding the paper down. Always make sure the safety cover is replaced after use.

A cutting surface

If you're using a craft knife, you will need something to cut on. Cardboard will do, but it must be thick. Rubber cutting mats are quite expensive, but will never wear out.

Most paper is colored on both sides – the blue figure is from paper of this kind. When this paper is torn, some of the edges will be a lighter shade and have a different texture. Try this yourself with cheap colored paper.

Some paper is colored on one side only, and is white on the back. The figure in pink is torn from paper of this kind. Try tearing a piece in half yourself. One of your torn strips will have a colored edge, and one will be edged with a dramatic white line. This can look very effective against a background of a different color.

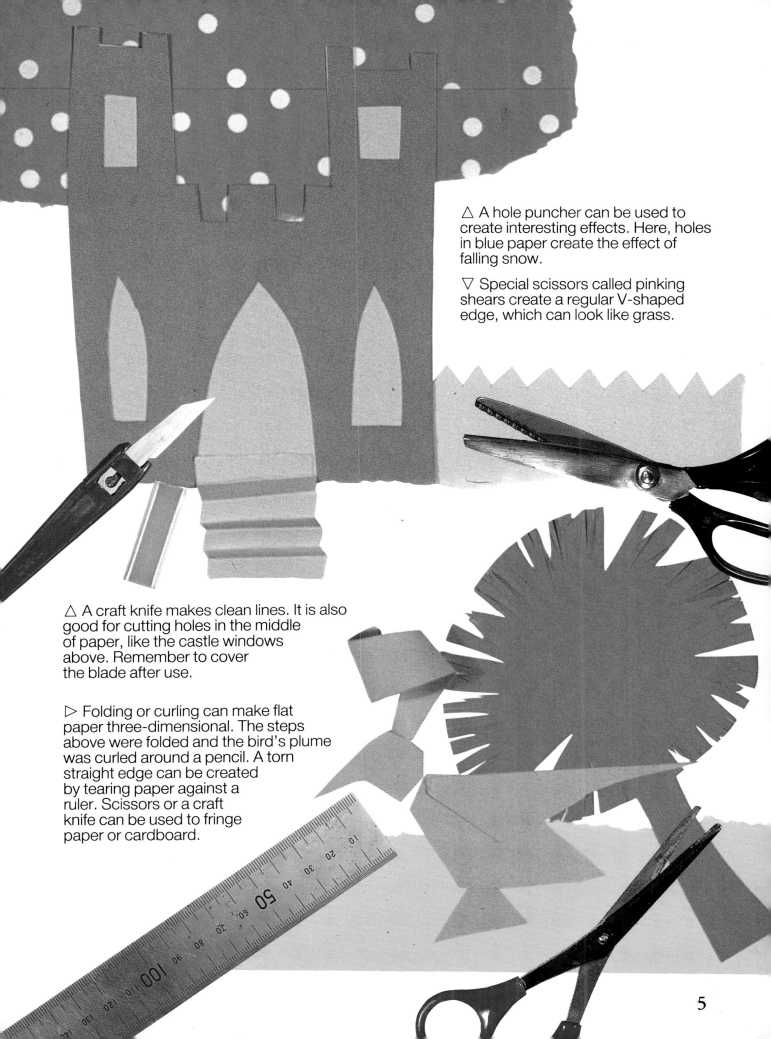

△ A hole puncher can be used to create interesting effects. Here, holes in blue paper create the effect of falling snow.

▽ Special scissors called pinking shears create a regular V-shaped edge, which can look like grass.

△ A craft knife makes clean lines. It is also good for cutting holes in the middle of paper, like the castle windows above. Remember to cover the blade after use.

▷ Folding or curling can make flat paper three-dimensional. The steps above were folded and the bird's plume was curled around a pencil. A torn straight edge can be created by tearing paper against a ruler. Scissors or a craft knife can be used to fringe paper or cardboard.

5

SPECIAL EFFECTS WITH PAPER

Paper is a very flexible material that can be used in all kinds of different ways. Some of the special effects you can achieve are described here; you may be able to think up some new ones of your own.

Changing texture

Paper usually has an even, uniform surface. But this **texture**, or feel, can be changed. Thin paper, such as tissue paper, can be crumpled and then flattened out again. Paper can also be pressed onto rough or textured surfaces to give it a different feel. This effect will be increased if you rub over the paper placed on a textured surface with a hard object like the back of a spoon.

With tin foil you can create the impression of an object by wrapping foil around it and then lifting it off. The spoon below is an example.

▽ *"The collage below uses a number of techniques to produce a picture of the objects found on a kitchen table. I crumpled purple tissue paper to imitate the wrinkled surface of prunes. To simulate the pitted surface of strawberries I pressed red paper over a sieve and rubbed it with a spoon. Sometimes the best way of capturing the look of an object is to include the object itself in your collage! The paper plate is an example."*

STICKING PAPER DOWN

Drawing and painting
Because it uses colored paper, one of the advantages of collage is instant access to large areas of color. You can also draw or paint parts of the paper to create a range of different effects. Colored pencils, crayons, chalks, felt-tip pens and paint can all be used for this.

Gluing paper down
Once your paper is torn or cut and painted, you will need to attach it to the background of your collage. Gluing is the basic method. Glue is available in liquid, paste and spray form, in pots, tubes or cans.

Different glues are right for different jobs. Most dry to a clear surface, and glue left showing can be rubbed away.

Tape, pins and staples
Tape can be used to stick paper down. Use double-sided tape on the back if you don't want it to show. Pins and staples can attach heavier papers to cardboard or styrofoam.

▽ *"Below is a fruit bowl collage made with a combination of cut and torn shapes, painted and stuck down in various ways. Thumbtacks and staples can become part of the picture – here I've positioned them to look like pips and stalks of fruit."*

THE WORLD OF PAPER

Paper is the single most important resource of the collage artist. From tissue paper to newsprint, from picture postcards to typing paper, it's important to get to know the range of papers that are available.

A library of paper

Start your own paper collection. You may be surprised by how much normally gets thrown away. Gather together a stock of paper that you can draw on for this project.

The aim is to find out what paper can do by putting together your own collage of flowers from different papers. Bring in as many textures as you can find. Sandpaper, envelopes and foil are used on the right.

Cut or tear yourself a series of petal shapes from your papers.

Practicing composition

If you pick or buy a bunch of flowers, you will probably want to arrange them in a vase at home. In the same way, your paper flowers need to be arranged in a pleasing way. This process is called composition. One of the great advantages of collage is the ability to practice composition, trying your materials in all kinds of positions before deciding on a final version. When you decide what looks best, stick them down.

▷ *"Don't forget you can overlap some of your flowers, as I have in the collage on the right. You'll find that using similar shapes will bring out the different qualities and textures of the paper."*

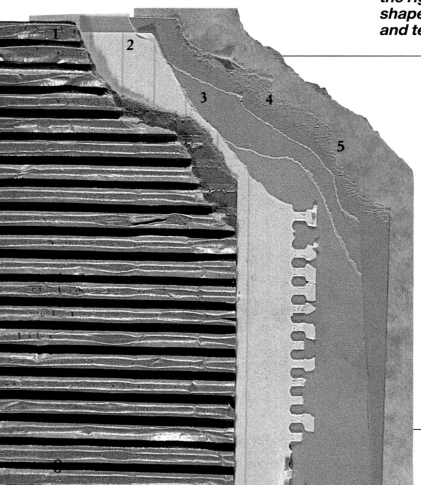

All about paper

Paper comes from trees. It's made from pulped wood mixed with water and pressed flat. Paper can have other substances, flax for example, mixed in with it to give it a different texture. Paper is available in many different weights and textures. Shown here are (1) corrugated paper (2) notepaper (3) tracing paper (4) construction paper and (5) wrapping paper. Construction paper is inexpensive and comes in many colors. Thick watercolor paper and cheap bond paper are also useful.

41

9

STEP BY STEP

Gathering your materials

The previous page explored the potential of paper in collage. But collage can also involve a much wider range of materials. This project is about working with more varied materials, and building a picture with them step by step.

Begin by assembling your raw materials. You might collect ready-made images, like postcards and photographs from magazines. You could also include construction paper (shown behind the magazine photographs on the right).

1

2

△ *"A mixture of torn and cut edges will add interest to your picture. Your paper shapes can be overlapped. Keep an open mind about where and at what angle the pieces might go."*

△ *"Magazine images add color and texture to your work. Remember that being able to make alterations to your pictures before or even after sticking them down is an advantage of collage."*

Finding a subject

If you are the sort of person who finds it easy to have ideas, a subject for your collage may come to you before you begin gathering your materials. Alternatively, as you make your collection, a theme that pulls them together may become clear. Sometimes it's easier to let your subject suggest itself to you, than to have a fixed idea before you start.

To begin your collage, cut and tear simple shapes for some of the key elements your theme suggests (1). Begin experimenting with these elements in different positions.

Size and scale

Postcards and photographs (2) provide ready-made images which allow you to experiment with size and scale. In real life, objects that are close to us look large, and those that are far away look tiny. You can recreate this effect in your collage with images of different sizes.

Look at the images of animals on the left. The largest, the lion, seems to belong in the front, or foreground, of the picture. The medium-sized gorilla looks right in the middle, and the tiny bird looks best at the top, where it appears to be in the distance.

Putting it all together

Now that your main materials are assembled, it's time to see how everything fits together (3). The elements of your collage are pieces of a puzzle that can be put together in different ways. There's no right or wrong way to assemble the pieces – it's about what looks best to you.

In the final stages, bring in the odds and ends of junk you collected earlier. These will add touches of interest, realism or even humor to your collage, and, most important of all, give it a three-dimensional look.

3

△ **"Above is the finished collage. A bottle top has become the sun, and a piece of string has turned into a snake sunning itself on a rock. A stronger glue was needed to fix these down securely."**

WORKING WITH COLOR

One of the joys of collage is being able to work with large areas of color, without first having to mix paint, or to crayon laboriously. There's no better way to find out how colors work together.

Colors have many jobs to do

Colors express feeling; they can create mood and atmosphere. Colors can blend together or stand out against each other. Colors influence one another; they can appear to change, depending on the other colors they are placed next to.

Colors can also suggest distance and space. Warm colors such as yellows and reds seem to jump out and grab your attention. Cool colors such as blues and purples are more relaxing. By positioning colors correctly, you can create a real sense of depth in your work.

Creating depth with color

This project will work best with transparent paper of different colors. Tissue paper is ideal; it allows colors to show through one another, so two different colors can be overlapped to make a third color.

Discover how to put colors in their place by building up a land- or seascape. Begin by laying down broad areas of color. Use warm colors in the foreground, and cooler colors in the background. Overlap your colors to create more subtle shades, like the turquoise at the water's edge in the collage shown.

▷ *"To get the tissue paper to lie flat, I put small spots of glue on either end of the torn strips and smoothed them down. When the background was finished, I added the details of the sun, boat and the bathers, to focus the eye on the different areas of the picture. "*

Warm colors advance toward you. They are right for the foreground of your picture. Cool colors recede; they fit best in the background.

The eye is drawn to contrasting colors such as yellow and purple, which demand attention. Other contrasting pairs are red and green, blue and orange.

A single layer of transparent yellow or red paper laid over a white background looks pale and muted; a double layer looks darker and brighter. Red and yellow are overlapped to make orange, as you can see in the middle below.

EXPLORING TONE

What is tone? Tone is about how light or dark something is. Take away color, and tone is what is left. Tone gives shape and solidity to objects, by showing where light falls on them. Reproducing this effect will make your work look convincing.

This project is about practicing seeing tone by making a collage in newspaper. Your subject could be a still life, like the one shown here.

Tone and lighting

Arrange some objects into a still life. Look closely at it. There are two factors that affect the tones there: the actual colors of your objects – how light or dark they are – and the effect of light falling on them. For example,

a pale highlight on a black jug could actually look lighter than a shadow on a white plate.

Matching tone

Study the effect of light on your arrangement and identify areas of tone in it. Match what you see with the black, gray and white tones of your newspaper. Cut or tear shapes from paper of the right tone, and slowly build up your picture.

▷ *"From the large black letters of the headlines to widely spaced lettering and small print, a newspaper contains all the tones you need for your still life. To make the job simpler, I put the background in first, and the paler shapes over it."*

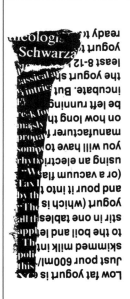

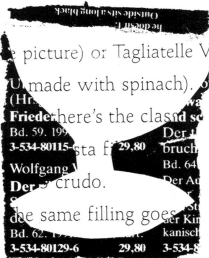
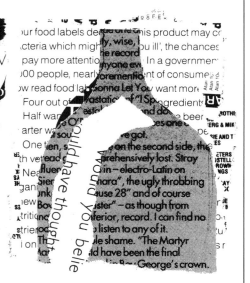

△ *"A light shining from the side creates areas of pale tone and shadow on an object. Sometimes these are very distinct."*

△ *"Placing light and dark tones next to one another produces a dramatic effect. The eye is drawn to these areas.*

△ *"Cut shapes convey abrupt changes in tone. A torn line can suggest one area of tone blurring into another."*

All colors have tones, too. If you look at the squares above, you may be able to identify particular colors, and the differences between their tones. Compare them to the tone of the page, and that of your hand holding this book.

MARBLING AND RUBBING

Marbling paper is fun, and can produce the most amazing results for you to use in collage. You will need oil paint, linseed oil, turpentine, a bowl and some jelly jars. Cover your working area with newspaper, and follow the instructions below.

Rubbings

Rubbings are impressions of textures in color. Look around you for objects with interesting textures. Place a sheet of thin paper over each, and rub the paper with colored crayon, pencil, or chalk.

▷ *"When you've produced a number of rubbings and marbled papers in different colors, study them and see what the different textures remind you of. Use them to make a collage, perhaps a landscape like the one on the right."*

△ *"In a jelly jar, mix up one teaspoonful of linseed oil with two of turpentine. Add six inches of paint squeezed from a tube, and stir the mixture with a stick."*

△ *"Make up several jelly jars with different colors. Fill a bowl with water. Pour in a jar of paint. The mixture will float on the surface of the water. Stir it again."*

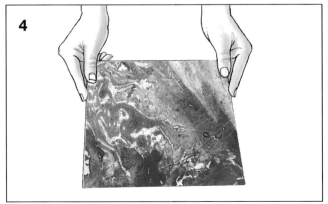

△ *"Take a piece of plain paper and gently lay it on the surface of the water. Lift it off again almost immediately, and let the excess water drain off. Lie it flat to dry."*

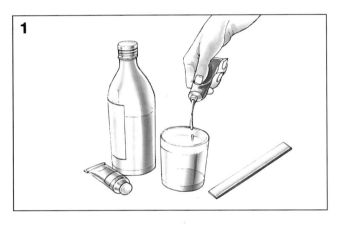

△ *"Your paper will now be marbled. You could immerse it again in a different color, or add a new color to the water and try again with a fresh sheet."*

16

Making a good impression

Below are some examples of different textures obtained by rubbing. Try rubbings of coins and the grain of wood.

Many kitchen utensils also have interesting textures – try a cheese grater, a sieve, and a straw place mat. You'll discover a new world at your fingertips!

WORKING WITH PHOTOS

"From this day on, painting is dead." Many people believed this when photography was first invented. Artists today haven't actually given up painting, but a great many have used photographs in picture making.

Picture puzzles
Cutting up and reassembling a photograph is a little like making your own jigsaw puzzle. This process will produce a new image which can be intriguing, bizarre or funny.

You will need a collection of images from postcards or magazines. These pictures can be cut up, using scissors or a craft knife. Cutting paper with a craft knife held against a metal ruler will produce a clean edge. There are many ways in which the pieces that you cut can be reassembled. A few are shown here, and others are suggested for you to try.

Squares, strips and fans
Photographs can be cut into squares, as described below, or they can be cut into straight strips or curves. Curved strips can be spread out evenly, or shaped into a fan. Fanning will elongate your image. On the right, fanning has emphasized the curve of the goose's neck. This technique is very effective with photographs of figures in action.

Two into one *will* go
Another project with strips is shown at the bottom of the opposite page. This project works best with two images that complement each other, as the shape of the bird's head and the hill do there. Cut both pictures into strips, and intersperse the two images. When the pictures are combined, the shapes will interact with one another.

◁ "The image on the left is composed of squares. To cut squares more accurately, mark out the lines on the back of your image first.
The illustration shows only one of the many ways in which the squares can be reassembled. Try rotating each square by 90°, and see what happens. Try again, rotating all the squares by 180° and sticking them upside down."

△ *"Here the photograph from the opposite page has been treated very differently. Try replacing strips like these in reverse order, or removing every other one and putting the rest together again."*

▽ *"The round hill echoes the shape of the bird's head below. Look for similar shapes for your own collage."*

PHOTOMONTAGE

A collage made up of a number of photographs is called a photo-montage. Photomontages can often look more like pictures of dreams than of everyday life. In dreams, familiar objects or people are often transformed into the unfamiliar, and sometimes the same thing happens repeatedly. In photomontage, too, shapes can be repeated, and familiar images can be transformed into strange and bizarre ones.

This photomontage project is about exploring the patterns you can make with repeated shapes. You will need a craft knife and magazines.

Repeating shapes

Look through the magazines and find an image that appeals to you. Choose a figure or a simple form that is easy to recognize from its outline or silhouette alone. Cut around the outline, pressing down hard on the magazine and cutting through several other pages as you do so. When you've cut out your outline, you will be left with a series of identical shapes (see the illustration below).

Positive and negative

You will also have a number of holes in backgrounds – negative shapes –

Front and back

On the left below, the figure has been cut out and moved from its original setting, leaving the negative shape.

On the right, both figures and backgrounds have been turned over, to produce a series of shapes which mirror those on the left.

as well as the positive ones of the figure itself. The idea is to use these shapes as well in your collage.

Magazines are printed on both sides of the paper, so your positive and negative images will have parts of other pictures printed on the back of them. These, too, can become part of your picture.

Once you have a series of images and backgrounds, start to experiment with them. Turn some over and see how they mirror the others. Put them all together in your own collage. The montage below is based on this mirroring technique, and also on the dreamlike transformation of one thing into another.

▽ *"In my photomontage, single leaves have transformed themselves into whole trees. A cat's face has become a butterfly; its shape echoes the floating features of the face on the opposite side."*

DRAWING WITH COLLAGE

Your work so far may have involved a certain amount of drawing or painting on collage paper. This project is about quite the reverse – incorporating elements of collage into a drawing or painting of your own.

Using collage fragments

Choose a subject for a drawing or painting – it could be a street scene like the one shown here, or the view from your window, perhaps. Take a fresh look at the newspapers and magazines you gathered earlier. Get your imagination working on how these fragments fit in. Alternatively, let your fragments suggest a subject. Newspaper headlines, patches of newsprint and magazine advertisements can all find new homes – you can see these in the collage on the right. Don't take the words on your fragments too literally – they don't need to correspond exactly to your subject to fit in well.

Mixing materials

The picture opposite was drawn in pencil, charcoal, brown oil pastel, and pen and ink. You could use some of these in your own picture. Leave spaces in your drawing for your collage fragments. When you finish, glue them in place.

▷ *"If your subject is a street scene, printed words and pictures can add a touch of realism to storefronts, signs or billboards. Collage can also help you turn a drawing weak spot to your advantage. If you find drawing people difficult, why not collage them in instead?"*

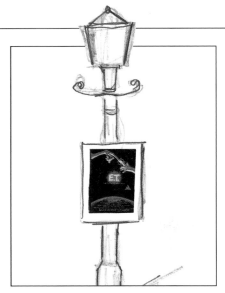

△ *"To avoid smudging, spray your drawing with fixative before you glue in your fragments."*

△ *"Alternatively, stick down your collage paper first, and draw an image around it."*

△ *"If you can't find a word, cut out separate letters and paste them down to spell it out."*

WORKING WITH FABRIC

You don't have to be able to sew or knit to enjoy the rich world of cloth. Fabrics open up an entirely new range of possibilities, enabling you to achieve effects you can't get any other way.

Many textures

Most households have a bag of cloth scraps tucked away. Collect as many different kinds of fabric as you can. Silk, corduroy, velvet, burlap, muslin – each material has its own unique character, a particular color, weave, texture and pattern.

Buttons, sequins, lace, yarn, and felt can all be brought in. You will also need a pair of sharp scissors, strong glue, pins or staples, and thick cardboard or cork to use as a base.

What do your scraps suggest?

Study your fragments and see what they remind you of. You could try a head like the one opposite, or an animal, landscape, or abstract pattern. Work as you have with paper, experimenting with your fragments in different positions before sticking or stapling them down.

▽ *"The odds and ends I collected suggested the crazy face and clothes of a clown. I chose pink nylon for the face and a background of cotton twill, and began by laying down these basic ingredients."*

▽ *"I chose shiny red cotton for the clown's nose, and small cotton patchwork squares for his jacket. I tried strands of yarn for the hair, but finally opted for a coarse tweed material."*

THREE-DIMENSIONAL COLLAGE

Throughout this book, in gluing one piece of paper over another, you have been creating an image which is actually three-dimensional. This project is about developing this quality fully, and creating an image that really stands out!

A load of old trash
You will need to make a new collection, this time of junk!

◁ *"Nails, pinecones, bark and the imprint of a car in foil have all been used on the left. The toys add interest and draw the eye to different parts of the collage."*

Old boxes, tubes, plastic bottles, toys, wood and leaves can all fit in. You will need a base of wood, cork or styrofoam. Nails, staples or glue can be used to fix objects to it.

Choose a subject or let your materials suggest one. You could try a science fiction city scene with stairways and towers, as shown here.

Using shadows
One of the advantages of 3-D collage is that the shadows cast by solid objects can become part of the design. When you're all finished, a coat of paint will unify your collage, and emphasize the play of light and shadow on it.

Adapting your materials
Some of your materials will need to be transformed before they can be used. Open out some boxes, cut into others; halve tubes and splay out plastic cups. Fold cardboard to make steps, cut doors and windows. Hide things inside others to be discovered at closer inspection.

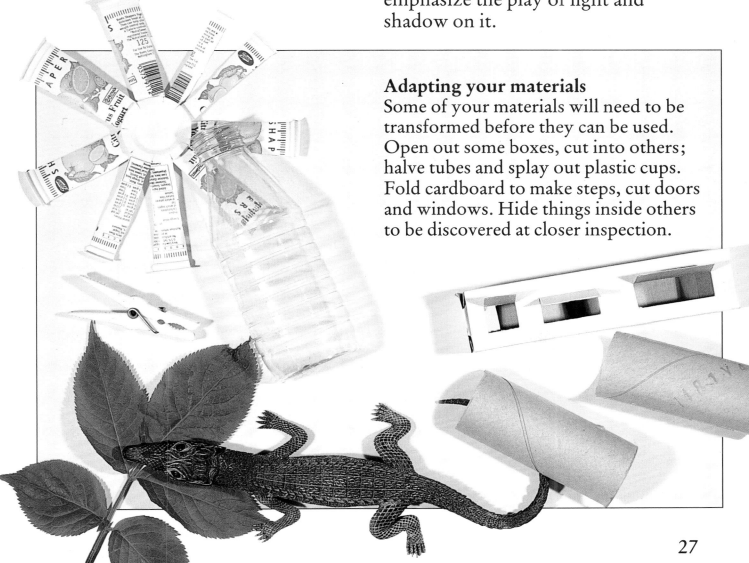

A DIARY IN COLLAGE

It's said that every picture tells a story. Have you ever kept a scrapbook of a vacation you went on, with all kinds of odds and ends that reminded you of the trip? This page is about using the bits and pieces connected with such a journey to make a collage. Again, the image you create will be three-dimensional.

Scrapbook journalism
In unknown territory, bus tickets and even candy wrappers can have a special magic. If you have an old scrapbook, this project provides you with an opportunity to recycle all your old vacation souvenirs. If not, you will need to go on a special expedition to gather your materials.

A trip to a gallery or museum, even a walk in the park can provide you with the inspiration you need.

On your expedition

Plan a journey in advance that is likely to yield the kind of materials you are looking for. On your trip, collect anything that might be effective in a collage, including tickets, maps, leaflets and postcards.

Take snapshots, or draw quick sketches. You could decide to stop regularly, every hundred paces for example, and note or pick up anything that looks interesting. The things you collect need not be just paper – balloons, coins, film and sand have all been used on the left.

Composing your materials

When you get home, arrange your materials on a large sheet of colored cardboard, or on a base of cork or styrofoam. Test out your objects in different positions. Try to plan another interesting journey, this time for the viewer's eyes as they wander over the surface of your collage. When you find the most pleasing composition, pin, stick or staple down your materials. Many modern artists have presented records of their journeys in this way.

◁ *"My collage records a trip to Disney World, but as you can see, the work is still in progress. Most of the materials have been positioned, but the objects bottom right have still to become part of the picture."*

Your own collage might include some of the materials below – brochures and postcards, maps, tickets and passes. You could also use "found objects" – twigs, leaves, flowers, earth, shells, and even packages of seasoning, as shown below.

GIFTS AND PRESENTATION

Collage offers a quick and easy way to produce all kinds of images in quantity. These images can make excellent cards and posters.

Repeating yourself

By pressing hard through several layers of paper with a craft knife, or by cutting several sheets at once with sharp scissors, you can create a series of identical shapes. These shapes can be used to mass-produce cards or posters. On the left are identical posters for a school play, which were made in this way.

Varying composition

Identical shapes don't have to be arranged in the same way every time. On the right are two party invitations made with identical materials. The pieces have been arranged in two very different compositions – shapes have been positioned at different angles, and even stuck in upside down. If you glue your paper shapes onto stiff cardboard, the final result will stand up and should last longer.

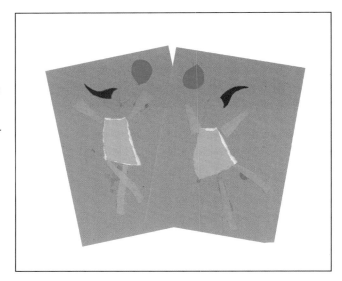

Presentation

Your collages will look even better when well presented. Some will look good with trimmed edges, mounted on cardboard or framed behind glass. If your collage is made of freely torn shapes, the rough edges may look best untrimmed, mounted with a border of cardboard on all sides.

PRACTICAL TIPS

Storing your materials

Many of the projects in this book have involved collecting materials. These need to be stored, if you wish to avoid the trouble of a time-consuming search every time you begin a new project. Organize some storage space for your materials. Sort different kinds of paper into separate piles, and file them away in a drawer if possible. If not, store them in boxes, trash can liners or plastic bags. If you can lie the bags flat, the paper will not get creased.

Preparation

You will also need to organize a work area. Whether you work on the floor or a table, you will need a lot of space. Collage is messy work, and in the heat of the moment, a certain amount of mess is inevitable. In fact, if you worry too much about making a mess, you probably won't be able to put so much enthusiasm into the project itself.

Before you begin, spread newspaper over the surface on which you intend to work. Wear old clothes. Keep tissues at hand to mop up spills or excess glue. Don't forget to replace the cap on your tube of glue, and to cover your craft knife when you have finished with it.

Gluing large areas

If you need to glue large areas of paper, wallpaper paste is ideal.

The paste should be mixed with water in an old bowl or jelly jar. You will need to apply it with a brush.

Warning

The fumes of some kinds of glue are harmful. Be very careful not to breathe them in.

More tearing techniques

Tearing is a direct and easy way of producing a shape in paper, but sometimes results may seem haphazard. You can achieve a more controlled tear by lightly scoring a line in your paper first with a craft knife or with the blade of your scissors. Tear along the scored line for a slightly ragged edge, or press out the shape instead.

Alternatively, draw the line you want with a paintbrush dipped in water, and then tear along it while the paper is still wet.

At a distance

Collages are pictures too, and they need the chance to be seen in their own right. Once your work has been framed or mounted, hang it on the wall where it can be seen from a distance. As you become familiar with your work over a period of time, you may notice things you want to change or reposition. One of the great advantages of collage is that additions and alterations are almost always possible.

INDEX

▷ *"Styrofoam, bottle tops, corrugated paper and string have all been recycled to produce this image of flowers on a windowsill."*

PRINTED IN BELGIUM BY
proost
INTERNATIONAL BOOK PRODUCTION